Job Interview Qu

MW01592919

Winning Guide to Answering Even the Toughest Interview Question With Ease and Landing That Dream Job

By Clark Darsey

circumstances is the author responsible for any losses, direct or indirect, which are incurred as a result of the use of information contained within this document, including, but not limited to, —errors, omissions, or inaccuracies.

Table of Contents:

Introduction

You have an interview for your dream job just around the corner? I don't doubt that you have all the necessary skills for doing the job successfully. However, there is one more skill which is about actually getting that job and this skill is very rarely taught in school.

We all remember our first job interview. For most people, it was probably a similar experience as riding a bike for the first time ever or trying to watch an episode of Modern Family sober. Needless to say, it probably didn't go too well and that's fine and it is nothing to be ashamed of or bummed out about. The first time you do anything is unlikely to be the best and it can only get better from that point forward.

When you went to the first job interview, you probably weren't prepared since you didn't know what to expect. Proper preparation will make you seem like a proper professional who is serious and who knows what he wants and will make you stand out among other candidates who haven't done their homework.

Preparation entails two areas. You should be prepared physically and mentally so that you look the part and that you stay calm and unflustered, but you should also be prepared to answer the most common questions which tend to appear during job interviews. The way to be successful with these questions is not by memorizing the script and only using that as an answer to the questions.

The more fun way to be prepared to answer these questions is to know what those questions are attempting to find out and what does an interviewer want to determine by asking a particular question. Canned scripted answers simply won't work in as well in every situation and context. By just having proper awareness and understanding, you won't actually have to waste time constantly trying to memorize answers since preparing for a job interview is quite different than preparing for a school exam. However, proper preparation is all this book is about.

Chapter 1: Preparation

For the day of the interview, it is recommended to show up around 10 minutes early instead of just showing up on time. You want to set the tone and set the impression that you are reliable and that you can be on time. If you're not exactly sure where the job interview takes place, then it is a good idea to go to that part of town a couple of days before the interview and to see where exactly do you have to go. This way you will know exactly where to go and how much time it will take you to get there. Trust me, there's nothing worse than not getting to the job interview on time because you don't know where to go and it makes you feel like a buffoon. You will also be a lot calmer and confident if you have a plan and if you know exactly what you're doing. You always want to have some room for error and you should be especially careful if the interview is conducted during the hours when the traffic is bad.

It is necessary to do the research the company and the role you're applying for so that you have an understanding of what you will be taking part in and in which way you can add value. To go a step further, it is recommended to use resources other than only the company website such as news or social media. After you have gone through this data, then you can see how your skills and knowledge and what you have put on your resume correspond to and fit in there. If you are given information on the person or persons who will be interviewing you, then it is a good idea to see if that person has a presence on Linkedin so that you could see who you are dealing with and be even more prepared. Just remember that people on Linkedin can see when someone views their profile, so you may want to be careful with this.

Getting enough sleep is generally recommended for every night, but it is especially important to get this right on the night before the interview in order to do your best during the interview. Don't eat anything in the evening that may compromise sleep and make sure that in your bedroom it is so dark that you can't see anything other than the blackness. The temperature in the room should be a bit on the cooler side. It is also not recommended to do anything stimulating an hour or so before bed or to be around many electronic lights. Electronic lights emit so-called blue light which is a wavelength which, when absorbed by the eyes, stops melatonin from being released, melatonin being the hormone which makes people sleepy during the times of the day when they usually go to bed. To combat this you can also have an application such as flux installed on your devices which will block most of that blue light. It is also a good idea to purchase blue light blocking glasses and to wear the hour or two before going to bed.

It is necessary to be dressed for the occasion and to have clothes and other documentation laid out and ready before the day of the interview so that you don't have to waste time and nerves. Things like your CV, certifications, list of questions you want to ask and all the rest should be prepared and all in one place. It's even good to be aware of what the weather will be like so that you know if you will have to make some necessary adjustments in order to reach the interview. You should be aware of the appropriate dress code and to not be below that. There is no need to overcomplicate this, the most important factor is that the clothes fit you well.

One thing to remember is that the interview starts as soon as you enter the building and you should try to leave a good impression on everyone. For example, the person on the reception may be under instructions to observe everyone who shows up for the interview, so anyone who treats the receptionist haphazardly will have their points taken away. How you do one thing is how you do everything. Also, when you're sitting or standing in the waiting room, that is the worst time to be checking your phone since you never know who is watching. Just be there and wait, there will be plenty of time for checking the phone later during the day.

When the interview starts, just have a relaxed and open body language. Don't be afraid to take a little bit of space since you will look more confident and adopting such a power pose does actually influence your mood and your confidence. Instead of just answering a question point blank, it is recommended to try to steer the interview into an actual conversation by telling a story which will most likely put everyone at ease. The interview should begin and conclude with a proper handshake while maintaining eye contact. Also, thank people for their time and for the opportunity for the interview. A lot of people don't even get that opportunity.

Chapter 2: Interview Questions and Answers

The following chapter contains the hard-hitting interview question and what you need to know about them so that you can answer them appropriately and show how you are the right person for the job.

Question Number 1: Tell Me About Yourself

If there is ever a question which will certainly be asked during an interview, it is bound to be this one. You can bet your house on this question being asked. It will likely be the first question which will be asked. There may be a variation such as: „Tell me more about yourself", although the answer for all those is the same.

The person asking the question has already seen what is on your resume and will not want to hear you repeat all those things again. You should keep your answer to this question concise and not go too much into details since that will just increase the chances of you saying something that interviewers may not want to hear or which they may interpret in the wrong way. The answer to this question should be purely professional without any personal info since this is most likely the first question which will set the first impressions.

The point you want to get across is why you are the right person for the position based on your experience, that is pretty much what is attempted to be found out by this question. Each and every question has a certain objective and what is attempted to be found out by asking it. You want to give a brief overview of your relevant professional career and of your responsibilities at each company you worked at. If there was a certain accomplishment during your previous roles which will improve your chances of landing this position, then make sure to mention it. You want to hint at how your knowledge and experience can help fulfill a need or solve a problem for your desired position and that will give interviewers and hiring managers an impression that you are actually trying to help instead of only looking out for yourself.

It is recommended to use as few words as possible in order to get to point across instead of rambling and going offtopic. People who can talk less, but better seem more trustworthy and less nervous since they stand behind their words. The answer should be like an elevator pitch which has to focus only on the essentials in a short time while it lasts. The ideal length of an answer to this question would be between 1 and 3 minutes. This question is actually more centered around evaluating the presentation skills and the different facets of presentation skills such as charisma and organization and likeability instead of the actual content of the answer. It's more about how you answer instead of what you answer. It should be answered clearly without stuttering and with somewhat of vocal variation. It is not recommended to have a memorized answer since it will sound a lot more natural and genuine that way and if you really do have a reason why you want that particular job, then there shouldn't be a problem since words will always come easy in such case.

It's always better to have certain points in mind and then to leave yourself some spontaneity in answering the question. This is the first question and the answer to that question should pique the curiosity so that the interviewers would want to continue with the interview. An example of an answer for an accounting job would be: „For the last however many years I've been working at X company where I've started at an entry position where I got the chance to learn and to build relationships. My organizational and project improvement skills have enabled me to advance and to get promoted to a position where I could take part in developing software which would improve our processes. It was a very good position and I would be contempt staying there and possibly getting to a management position, but I was intrigued with the direction you were taking with your business and I wanted to have a chance at contributing towards that vision with my creativity and my organizational skills. I do believe I have the necessary skills and I am willing to learn what I may not know at the moment but will need to know for doing the job."

Question Number 2: What Do You Know About Our Company?

This is another common interview question and what interviewers don't want to hear is you regurgitating statistics or something you have found on top of their website. The main thing which is attempted to be found out by this question is whether you understand what the company is trying to accomplish and if you can actually understand what is being said in vision and mission statement. You should be able to read between the lines of vision and mission statement and to be able to relate that to your own values. Employers will always prefer someone who has a concrete reason for wanting to be part of a company instead of someone who is simply there because the position is open and available. Remember, it's better to know a couple of important facts really well instead of memorizing 20 different facts and making a whole bunch of mistakes in the process. The most important things to know are about what is the company best known for, what are the products or services etc.

Only a person who is really interested in the position will actually be able to give a proper answer to this question since they actually took the time to do the research past the surface. Such a person will probably appreciate the position an the chance to work there a lot more. Answering this question the proper way will carry you much further than simply memorizing and reciting the sale figures and milestones and awards. What interviewers want to find out with this question is if you're one of the people who will send applications to 200 different places and treat each one the same since those are the kind of applicants they are reluctant to hire. You should mention something about that company which resonates with you and what is something that made you apply. This question attempts to separate people who are serious from those who would be only short term hires since it does cost to advertise a job and to conduct all the interviews.

One example of an answer to this question would be: „I know that you are one of the most respected accounting services in our country and that you were founded in 2010. after the realization about how many businesses fail because they don't pay close enough attention to the number and small details early on and they only notice those things when the consequences are possibly too high to mitigate. The founding person recognized this need and that's why the company has managed to grow so much over time.“

Question Number 3: Where Do You See Yourself In 5 Years?

The number of years which is mentioned in this question can vary, but it is not all that relevant and the answer will be the same regardless. By asking this question it is attempted to find out if you have any long term goals and something to work towards and if you are planning to stick around long term since hiring and training new employees costs time and money. It is still possible to answer this question without being too specific which is ideal if you're not interested in staying in that particular company for that long.

You still should have your answer ready which won't tip them off to the fact that you don't necessarily plan on staying at that particular company for 5 years or that you are planning on having a business in the future. Giving a general answer to this question is the ideal option since for most people the specifics of the answer to this question probably change every two months, I know it is so for me. No one really knows what the future holds and all those fancy 5-year business plans are nothing more than best case scenario estimates. It is more important to be aware of the core underlying reason for doing something instead of dwelling on the mechanics. The most important qualities you should convey through your answers are signs of ambitions and willingness to use a particular position to achieve growth.

The example of the answer to this question should be about where this position could take you and it could sound something like this : „I would be really happy with this position since in 5 years I would like to be considered as an expert in digital marketing which should be possible if I take this role seriously enough and that would allow me to work on more interesting and challenging projects and to possibly coordinate with other departments when I feel I am up to that task and to the responsibility "

Question Number 4: Why Do You Want This Job?

The synonym question to this question would be why do you want to for them or why do you want to work there. In either case, when the hiring manager wants to know that there is a reason why you've applied for that one specific job instead of using the same application template for every job out there. They also want to ensure that there are reasons other than money and that there is an overall purpose. It's perfectly fine if you're doing this to advance yourself and to make yourself more valuable, but what employers really love to hear is if you resonate with the companies cause and what company contributes to the world and they want to find out what is that you can do for them.

This is yet another opportunity to show how you've done your research about the company and how you know what you're getting yourself into. Every company has a certain culture and hiring managers are trying to find out if a certain person fills into it. Some praise is good to include, but not too much so that it wouldn't come out as fake. When you do give praise, it shouldn't be about the location or about the benefits, instead, it should be about products or reputation. Even though it is generally recommended to keep calm and cool during interviews, this is a question where showing some enthusiasm would go a long way. If possible, it can be a good idea to have a certain story which would reveal some connection even if that story is made up and you've never bought anything from a company. This is shown in an example answer.

Example of an answer to this question would be: „I have been a customer of your company for a while and I am happy with the products to the point where I want to contribute to making them even better. I really admire your way of putting customer service first since I have always been someone who likes to help people and for that reason, I am confident I would fit in well here."

Question Number 5: What Are Your Strengths?

For answering this question successfully, you should have a good understanding of the job description so that you know what qualities are required in order to do the job well. This question is trying to determine if you've done your research and if you have a good reason for applying for the position. If you can think outside of the box and think of some additional qualities which may not be traditionally considered for the position, then you can get bonus points.

It is ideal if you have an example of you utilizing your strengths to solve a problem or to handle a difficult situation. You should have a list of your strengths and skills which are relevant for the position and you shouldn't do anything more than a simple list since canned answers are the worst thing you can use. It is best to only focus on a couple of most important and relevant strengths in order to keep the answer concise and focused.

If the question is about your greatest strength, then you should focus on just one which you consider to be most important. You should avoid general and cliche strengths such as being a hard worker or determined or enthusiastic because just saying that will probably make interviewers roll their eyes. Those general strengths are the things which should be demonstrated without telling. It's better to be specific while being mindful of the position you are applying for. For example, it is better to say you are good at Facebook advertising for B2C instead of just saying that you are good at advertising. Framing things in this way also makes you sound more professional and trustworthy and like someone who knows what he or she is talking about.

An example of a good answer to this question would be: „My greatest strength would be writing sales copies which is something I would attribute to my book reading habit which has made me better at reading between the lines and figuring out how to make people interested. Thanks to that, I've managed to increase sales of company XYZ by 20% in the year 2016 and by 23% in the year 2017. While working there, I had to work with other people in order to complete projects which have made me better at working together with people which is very useful since I am aware of the fact that my work at this company would require a lot of that."

I hope that you are enjoying the book so far and hopefully this information will help you get the job that you want. If you want to share your thoughts and comments about this book, then you can do so by leaving a review on the Amazon page.

Question Number 6: What Are Your Weaknesses?

Thankfully, this question isn't asked very often and it does actually take a certain kind of person to actually bless someone with this question. This question is actually a waste of time since they're the focus is on what you can't do at the moment instead of what you can do for the company now. The more common and reasonable question to ask is about strengths since if you only focus on fixing your weakness all day then at the end of the day all you will have will be a bunch of strong weaknesses.

Nevertheless, it is still necessary to be prepared and to not bank on this question not appearing. The worst thing is to say that you have none which is more common for newbies and it simply shows the lack of self-awareness. For any weakness you decide to tell them about, you should say how you are working on improving it and you could also tell about the positive results of you deciding to take action of improvement. If you can really do a good job with only one weakness, then that will likely be enough and you won't have to list multiple weakness and you will be able to get this question out of the way as soon as possible.

You should stay away from using weaknesses such as impatience because those are personality traits. I believe that personality traits can be fixed and turned around and for more on this topic it is advisable to read Mindset by Carol Dweck, but this takes a lot more time than simply improving a skill so it is unlikely that employers would see some noticeable improvement while you are at the job. On the other hand, weaknesses in terms of skills or work ethic or organizational skills are something which can be improved reasonably quick and improvements can be visible with the naked eye much sooner.

It is also recommended to use weaknesses which only appear in a certain situation instead of something which is consistent. An example would be certain weakness appearing such as situational impatience only when a deadline is in question. Using a strength as a weakness may have worked before, but more and more people are catching on this way to get out of this answer and when you try to do that today, then people may get the impression that you would be dishonest and indirect and that you would try to weasel yourself out of situations as soon as possible. The typical example of this would be someone saying how they work too hard or how they are a perfectionist.

One example of an answer to this question is: „I tend to be too focused on the details and for that reason it can be hard for me to let things go or to delegate because I want everything to be just right, but I have realized over time that it is better for everyone if things can be organized in a way that everyone can work on things they are really good at so that more efficiency can be achieved. Related to this, it can also be hard for me to start since I can get lost in planning.“

Question Number 7: Why Should We Hire You?

The reason this question may be asked is that interviewers by that point aren't exactly sure about what makes you a better choice than the other candidates and what remains is one final push. This question will in a way test out your sales skills. The interviewers want to know that they have made the right choice considering what is required for a certain job position.

 Researching the company beforehand will give you a better understanding of what problems they may be dealing with and how you can add value. You can prove your value by having some of the results of your previous work printed out so that you can hand them out if necessary. These printed out results should demonstrate a certain problem and the results which you managed to generate as the result of your actions. You do not need to include all the small technical details on the print, but you should mention them during this question which will make you seem more competent.

 It is also good to include a story during this which can highlight how you demonstrated a certain key requirement for the position since stories are what people remember more. Here you should focus on a few things which you can do really well which are ideally required for doing the job well. To find this out, you can ask the people who you worked with before to tell you honestly. The simple answer of you being a hard worker won't cut it since anyone can say that. More depth and thoughtfulness is required for this answer.

The example of a good answer to this question is: „Last year at my previous job, we were creating a social media marketing plan and I did my part by designing the approach for the younger demographics since I seemed to understand their habits and their technology use the best. I can also do the same for you since there is a huge opportunity in offering your products and services to younger potential customers as well."

Question number 8: Tell Me About A Time When You Handled A Difficult Situation

By asking this question, the interviewers are attempting to figure out your problem solving and critical thinking skills and the ability to work well with other people and to be flexible and adaptable as the situation changes. This question also attempts to measure creativity which is really important if the position you are being interviewed for requires creative work. The interviewers are also trying to see how well can you handle conflict since some will say that a person's true character is revealed then. Every employee is a representative of the company, so it is obvious why a company would want to uphold a respectable image. Of course, not all workplaces will have the same possibility of conflict, but this is still a reasonably common question.

The answer to this question will work best if you have a story example which will demonstrate the problem and the actions you took in order to reach the solution and the positive result. You should also state how you learned from the experience and how it has enabled to be even more effective in the future. The problem should be something that's happened in a workplace setting and it is a bonus if a deadline and other people's emotions are included since you will look better if you have managed to diffuse and to handle such a situation. It is still not recommended for this to be about some petty coworker issue, it should be about work specifically.

An example answer to this question is: „When I was working in a retail job a customer came wanting to return a malfunctioning tablet she bought the other day and to get another one. Even though my work day was minutes from being over and I just wanted to go home, I patiently listened to customer's request and after checking the stock it turned out that there were no tablets available in that store or in any nearby stores so it turned out that we would have to request supplies from another town over meaning that she couldn't get a working tablet on the spot. I did find out that the resupply run was due that same day which meant that the tablet which she wanted could arrive today. Knowing that, I apologized to the customer which I immediately followed up with a request for her leaving her contact info and her address so that the item could be delivered to her doorstep and it conveniently all matched up so that she got the tablet delivered the same day."

Question Number 9: What Is Your Dream Job?

While asking this question, an interviewer wants to know if you are really motivated about this job since such people will perform much better. People asking this question also want to find out if you will like this job and if they will like you once you are in and does it even make sense for you to be in a certain job position. The interviewer also wants to know if you have proper expectations concerning your job search. If you are applying for the receptionist job, then it is probably not the best idea to mention the aspiration of becoming a director. If you talk about the opportunities and responsibilities which could never be a part of the job you are applying for, then that will be a red flag for the interviewing staff. It is actually ok if the job you are applying for is not your dream job because it is better to answer this question in a general manner instead of describing a job title.

When answering this question, it is better to be general and to talk about things such as the work culture and the challenges and the skills which you are using and want to improve on. If you apply for customer service role, then it will be better to say that is is your dream to help people and to make people happy instead of taking calls and answering emails since the latter simply sounds ridiculous. It is better to talk about ambitions and goals and how the particular job might get you closer to that. This is actually a question where it is appropriate to talk about what the job can do for you instead of what you can do for them, although you shouldn't go too far and crazy with this.

An example answer should have to be general and should be modified to fit into what is actually done at the job and the example of such an answer is: „My dream job would be participating in designing products and services which make a positive difference in people's lives and also helping those products and services get out there into the world. People are benefiting every day by using your products and I would like to do my part to provide even more value."

Question Number 10: What Other Companies Are You Interviewing With?

When hearing this question it is important to slow down and to never mention the names of any companies you actually sent applications to. Even if the recruiter wants to know about the names of the companies, it is completely within your rights to politely decline to disclose any names. The thing is that a lot of hiring managers are actually well connected and the last thing you want is to discuss your particular situation with hiring managers of other companies. If they probe for names, the most you should tell them is that the companies are similar to what they do and that you wouldn't say that you are being interviewed at that particular company even if it was asked by hiring manager of another company.

If you actually give out names, then the hiring manager may call that company and tell them how poorly you did on an interview even if did well. The fact is that companies don't want to let good talent go since it is rare. This all may come as a revelation to some people, but this is actually happening behind the closed door. You can answer that you are interviewing for several other companies and that the interview process is near its end since this will instill a sense of urgency which will work even better if you are proving to be a desirable candidate.

After saying that you are being interviewed for other positions you can state a particular reason why you were attracted to their company and in that way redirect the conversation and end that question. You shouldn't say that you aren't interviewing anywhere else since that won't make you seem like a desirable candidate and like someone who is in demand. Employers want someone who is in demand so that they wouldn't regret their choice later on. It's pretty much the same reason why people look at reviews before buying anything. Even if you had zero interviews so far, you still want to make it sound like had. What you do want to show is that you are applying for a job similar to that companies since you won't seem like someone who is desperate sending out dozens of applications and willing to take anything that is offered. By applying for all kinds of position, there is a sense that a person doesn't really know what they want. Success isn't attracted by desperation.

An example of an answer to this question would be: „I am actively taking part in interviews for digital advertising agencies such as yours. It is going well and the roles I am primarily interviewing for are the ones which require expertise in Google Adwords.“

Question Numer 11: Why Are You Leaving Your Current Job?

There are many reasons for leaving certain jobs that don't have to do anything with money and some of those reasons can be toxic work environment or any other reason which may be perfectly legitimate, although none of these reasons should be mentioned to hiring managers because that would kill any chance of getting a job since you would give off an impression that you would be badmouthing that same job after you inevitably go looking for some other job.

As much as you would like to do that, try to avoid mentioning your previous jobs in a negative light. Make sure that the interviewing staff sees you in a positive light since first impressions go a long way When you do decide to give an answer to this question, remember that it is not necessary to go into details. It is better for everyone if you lean towards a general answer for this question that doesn't implicate any specific person. Never say that you are leaving because of differences and misunderstanding with the manager and the staff even if that may be true, it is more advisable to say that you feel that you have given all that you can and that you don't see any way up or the opportunity for the advancement.

One possible reason you were let go is because of the layoffs or restructuring or budget cuts or something similar. This is something that is out of your control and it doesn't have to do anything with performance. If this was the reason for the job loss, then simply explaining that will be all that the hiring manager needs to hear in order to conclude this question and move on to the next.

Regardless of the reason that isn't layoff-related, an all-around good example of an answer would be: „Even though I am happy with my current job, I have recognized that it is time to move on. I am grateful for the opportunity that was given to me there which allowed me to learn and to make myself someone who can provide more value. Seeing the role which this company is offering, I am confident that I could use what I know and what I can do to be a valuable part of an organization."

Question 12: How Would Your Boss And Your Co-workers Describe You?

By asking this question, the interviewers may attempt to get a bit more honest answer since it is easier for a person to exaggerate when talking about himself/herself. They also want to determine if you would fit well into the company culture. When answering this question you should be aware of job requirements and qualifications. Regardless of the job which someone is applying for, people want to make sure that the person they pick is nice to be around and easy to work with and a team player.

If you are applying for a customer service role, then it is recommended that you say that your colleagues would describe you as approachable and easy to talk to. Anyone can say this, however, and it is necessary to provide examples in order to really answer this question successfully. If you have a reference to back up your claim, that is even better. Think back of the times when you were commended for your work or about your performance reviews. When answering this question it is better to stay away from phrases such as „I think" or „I would" since those phrases convey less confidence and certainty. To start answering this question it is best to have some phrase ready after which you would list your relevant strengths with examples. You can start by using phrases such as: " In my previous job I was knows for..." or „My coworkers and/or bosses told me...."

A good example of an answer to this question is: „My colleagues told me on several occasions that I have good organizational and time management skills, which is actually why we managed to complete several important projects within a deadline. (Now you can describe those projects a bit). We actually managed to complete those projects way ahead of time which left us with more than enough time to do checkups and error assessments."

Question Number 13: Why Was There A Gap In Your Employment?

There are many reasons because of which the gap may exist. Everyone has them in today's world and it is not something which you should be ashamed of, it is just necessary to answer in a way which will ensure that nothing is held against you. If the interview overall is done properly, then the gap isn't something you should be too concerned with. One way to minimize the chances of this question being asked is to design a resume around your skills and achievements instead of work history and duration. It's not about hiding the gap, it's just about not putting it front and center.

Taking time off work to take care of sick family member is one of the reasons which interviewers won't probe for details and if that is the case, then you do not need to say anything more than necessary about that. Other reasons for the gap may be because you took time off to travel or to study or it may be because the job search wasn't going so well at the time because there weren't jobs available. Other real reasons may be because you were recovering from a previous bad job or if you took an overall break from employment or if you decided that you don't want to work in a certain industry anymore which may be the case, but it is not something which should be mentioned.

If you've been doing any relevant work and helping out with projects, then it is necessary to emphasize that so that the hiring staff wouldn't get an impression that you were doing nothing but sitting on a couch and playing Xbox all day. It is necessary to include anything which would give the impression that you were busy and using your time wisely, taking additional classes and volunteering and doing freelance work are great examples.

Take some time to compile a list of all the things you were doing at the time of the gap which could be seen as a positive contribution towards you being the better candidate for the job. At the end of the day, the interviewers care the most about the relevant skills for doing a good job and they may be trying to make sure that those skills haven't atrophied due to inactivity. Saying that you've been taking some online classes is the great way to convince them that they won't have to waste much time getting you into the action and showing you the ropes. You want to show that your skills are just as good as the other candidates even if you may have been without a steady job recently. Employers will usually focus only on the most recent gaps so there is no need to worry about the gap that occurred way back in time because it may be that you were in a completely different industry at the time.

The answer should be short and honest without necessarily going into storytelling mode. If the reason for being without a job is restructuring, relocation, lack of advancement opportunities or anything similar, then that may increase the interviewer's sympathy towards your situation. An example of an answer to this question is: „During my previous job I was doing only contract work instead of being a full-time employee, so when the contract came to an end, there simply wasn't any further need for my services. During the gap, I took some additional classes to brush up on my skills and I also did some freelance work in order to have some form of income. Juggling all those things has helped me improve my time management and organizational skills which will without a doubt come in handy in my future career."

Question Number 14: What Are Your Hobbies And Interests Outside of Work?

By asking this question, the interviewer may try to get some understanding about you and if you would be the person they would want to work with. A lot can be determined about a person based on the life outside the workplace. General hobbies such as going to the gym and listening to music are good answers, but many people use those and for that reason, it can be hard to stand out by using those examples.

It is ideal if the hobby can convey some qualities which can be valuable for doing the job itself. If you say that you play basketball with your pals couple of times per week and that you have also participated in some local competitions, then that can communicate that you can work well as a team member and that you also result oriented and competitive since you participated in the competition. If you go to the gym, then it is also good to mention some details such as the fact that you go three times a week since you will sound more determined and serious that way. That way it also doesn't sound like you made that up on the spot. Reading books is also a good hobby, especially if it is about an industry or a field you are interviewing for. Reading industry blogs or articles will do as well, although books are generally the most quality kind of content since bloggers will rarely go really deep into a topic.

It is not a bad idea to include something which would show that you are serious about a career. If you are volunteering and doing some charity work, then this is also good to mention since it will show that you don't care only about yourself. Be prepared for interviewer asking you to tell him or her a bit more about the hobby and why do you do it. This is a good opportunity to show some enthusiasm and instead of just saying that you listen to music, you can also say why you like to listen to music and what do you get out of it. Even if you like partying and drinking or online gambling, it is best not to mention that since that can make you seem a bit too immature for the position.

This question can be answered in many ways, however, an example of an answer to this question is: „I like going the gym, I feel that it really helps my discipline which can carry over to other areas of my life. I also like reading since actually sitting down and reading trains the ability to focus on one task without distractions.“

Question Number 15: How Well Do You Work Under Pressure?

It may be tempting to just answer this question with a yes and call it a day, but anyone can say that and it isn't telling the interviewer much, so for that reason you do need examples of when you had to meet a deadline or something similar in your previous jobs which also had a positive outcome in the end so that you would be remembered as such. There is no need to have more than one example as long as it is a good one, you should just make sure to connect it to you being able to perform well under pressure. Even if you're not the best at handling simultaneous responsibilities, it is still better to come across in a positive light by giving a general answer. Stress in the workplace is unavoidable, so the interviewers want to see if you can handle it and keep your cool in the future. It is even better if you have some go-to strategies which you use when needed.

An example of a good answer to this question is: „During my time at company XYZ, things were set up in a way which ensured that projects are delivered according to a strict deadline. This wasn't easy in the beginning, but with more experience and training from my superiors, I managed to get used to it and become more organized which lead to me not missing a deadline."

Question Number 16: How Did You Hear About This Position?

When asking this question, interviewers want to determine if you are an active or passive job seeker which will, therefore, determine your enthusiasm and your performance. Make sure that you don't give a quick answer saying how you heard about it from a friend, even if that may be the truth because there may be a policy in place which would prevent employees from talking to their friends about the position. In most situations, you shouldn't mention any names.

A lot better source to use is the ad in the newspaper or online and you should also remember the publication in which you saw the ad so that you could share that with the interviewer. Being redirected towards a position by a recruiter is also one of the possible channels. Just don't say how you don't remember how you came across the job opening since you will seem disorganized and like someone who is randomly sending dozens of applications. You should also try to connect that to your interests and passions and to what that particular company is doing as part of its business that made you interested in a position This all portrays you as an active job seeker who has put some real thought into your future.

A good answer to this question would go something like this: „I always had an interest in cars and, therefore, I am subscribed to several magazines. In this months article in XZ, there was a story about the latest project you are working on which led me onto your companies website where I was delighted to see a job opening which would give me an opportunity to be directly involved."

Question Number 17: Are You A Leader or a Follower?

I know that the first instinct may be to say how you are a leader since it may sound like a good thing that the hiring manager may want someone who can undertake responsibility, but it is important to remember what job you are interviewing for and what do the interviewers want to hear because what interviewers actually want to find out is if you can flexible and willing to adapt based on the companies needs. If you do say that you are a leader, then it is necessary to be prepared for a follow-up question where examples are expected such as projects or other situations.

It is also good to have some past examples of being a follower since the company wants someone who can follow directions instead of doing things on their own. It is not necessary to have a title in order o be a leader, it is enough to be really good at what you do so that people seek you out when they need help with a certain topic. Off course, when interviewing for some position such as staff, it is obvious that there won't be leadership duties, but it is still possible to work well together with people and to inspire while still following directions and orders like a follower would. Even when you are applying for a simple staff job, you still don't want to come across like someone who will just sit there and do things routinely without much thought. It ultimately depends on the situation if you are a leader or a follower and you will be both at different times.

A sample answer to this question could be something like this: „In my previous jobs, I was able to adapt to what the situation demanded. I could be a leader if that was necessary, However, I do realize that sometimes it is necessary to let some else who may be more knowledgeable on the topic take the lead."

Question Number 18: What Are Your Salary Expectations?

Even if you know your value and what you are worth, you have to avoid just giving a certain number since you don't know what you will exactly be doing and about a whole lot of other factors such as training, vacation time, benefits etc. By giving a number you will rarely get it right since you will either give too low of an amount and give off an impression that you don't think you are worth much or you will give too high of a number which may frustrate the hiring staff.

Giving a range is also not advised since that is almost the same as giving out a number since the hiring people will be focused on the lower end of that range and set that as an anchor. You don't want to give a range since people will then focus on the low and of the range and if it is possible for the employer to pay you less, then they will do that since that will mean fewer costs for them and therefore more profit. The people interviewing you and asking this question will rarely be the people who are making the final decision about the salary, so it is not necessary to worry too much about this question being asked. The people hiring you probably already have a salary they are planning to pay based on the budget and that won't likely be a subject to change.

It is better to answer this question in a general way saying that you like to be aware of the overall value of being a part of a certain company which extends to people you are working with, opportunities, the schedule and all the other factors which you are more informed about at the end of the interviewing process since at the moment your knowledge is limited which would prevent you from making an educated and informed choice. You should try to get across that compensation isn't the most important thing to you even if it may be and you should try to convey how adding value is actually a priority for you. By not answering this question right away, you would actually be putting yourself in a position to give a more educated and informed answer in the future.

If you want to play it safe, you can simply say that you expect to be paid an amount appropriate for your position and responsibilities and such an answer would convey that you did your research and that you know your worth. It's all about knowing your value since you are there to provide value, as catchphrasey as that sounds. You shouldn't worry about not giving a concrete number here as long as your resume and your requirements are on the required level. By providing the answer which demonstrates your value. This answer should be short and to the point and after you answer it, you should just stop talking and stand your ground and not give in if they push for the number. The final number is actually determined when the offer is on the table and you should hold out and stand your ground until that moment. Politely declining the direct answer does require some assertiveness and it is necessary to practice this since doing it correctly is sure to win you respect.

Question number 19: Would you rather be liked or feared?

Being decent may win you many companions at work yet you may finish up being a doormat for individuals to mistreat you. Then again, imparting fear into others to complete things can be powerful however your reputation will most likely take a hit So in case you're asked the mentioned question amid a job interview, how might you reply?

The inquiry isn't what it appears, same as most of these questions. the hiring chief most likely needs to find out your style of leadership and see whether you have integrity or not.

You are the better off by saying: „I'd rather be respected."

This is one of a handful of examples where it's totally fine to dodge the inquiry at hand as long as you understand what is attempted to be found out by asking this question. A few interviewers won't acknowledge this and press for a more concrete answer.

In the event that you were pressed to pick another answer, you could say: "I would prefer to be liked, in light of the fact that I trust that individuals make a special effort to assist those they do like, which will ensure that more people are working toward a common goal or a vision. I think fear is too negative a feeling and it doesn't enable a situation that is imaginative, inventive, or rousing to work to greatness."

One another example of an extended answer to this question could be: „Gee, well I surely wouldn't have any desire to be feared. I think fear is a horrendous inspiration: individuals are frequently feared if they are not being rational or if they are acting for an eccentric reason and for their own personal gains. I certainly don't work that way and I wouldn't want for anyone to get the impression that I do."

Question number 20: What motivates you?

This is a wide and open inquiry, which can make it difficult to realize how to reply. All things considered, the vast majority are moved by numerous variables, including pay, distinction, having any kind of impact, getting results, and cooperating with fascinating individuals.

By replying in a fair and mindful way, you can leave a good impression on your interviewer and show that you are the ideal individual for the job position.

By asking this question, the interviewers would like to make sense of what really matters to you. The enlisting supervisor needs to recognize what pushes you toward success. The person in question additionally needs to decide if what drives you will be a fit for the activity obligations and the organization culture as a whole.

Legitimate answers can help uncover what conditions enable you to feel energized and enthused and that is why another common version of this question can be: "What are you passionate about?". Asking this is an attempt to figure out what makes a candidate energized and satisfied. Giving knowledge into the powers that spur you at work can be a window into your identity and style, helping your questioners comprehend you as both an individual and a potential representative.

All things considered, there's a major distinction between the interviewees who are inspired by building groups and setting up solid associations with collaborators, while the person whose ideal day is chipping away at a report that enhances the organization's main essence. The two candidates with them solid focal points, and this question can enable questioners to limit their pool down to the person who is the most suited for the position and the organization.

The answer doesn't have to be outlandish, an answer just like the following can do the trick: „I've always enjoyed technology and math. There's no concrete reason for it, it's just what I enjoy doing. I wouldn't want to imagine doing something else as my career."

Question number 21: Tell Me About a Time When You Demonstrated Leadership

Regardless of what your major is or your career path, one of the most widely recognized questions you'll experience amid a job interview is "In which way have you demonstrated leadership?" When businesses pose this question, this is with the intention of wanting to get familiar with your identity and how you approach difficulties. They need to know whether you can step up and lead successfully when the event calls for it.

Talk about a time when you took on a role of the leader. The most ideal approach to do this is by reviewing a positive, brief case of a period when you showed initiative and doing your best to illustrate the circumstance. For instance, if you hosted a charity of some sort and collected a great deal of cash, make certain to make reference to that.

On the off chance that you can't think about an applicable example from a past job or temporary position, utilize a personal affair, for example, a period when you showed initiative while volunteering, taking part in clubs or sports or handling a scholarly undertaking.

Feature your achievements quantifiably. Anybody can think of a notable idea, however not every person can act on it. This is the reason it's vital to wrap up your answer by demonstrating how you attempted to achieve (and perhaps surpass) your objective. On the off chance that you can, talk about numbers. It's not hard to state that you made something into a success with no genuine method to gauge the result, yet on the off chance that you can you should demonstrate that you were effective, for example by demonstrating that the occasion you arranged raised a certain amount of money, that is a solid example which your future boss would love to know about.

Show that you're a cooperative person who can complete things. Nobody needs a leader who will just barge in, assume responsibility and afterward not really follow up. Indeed, it's critical to have somebody managing a venture, but on the other hand, you should be able to demonstrate that you can get down to work. While laying out the means you took to accomplish your objective, make sure to discuss your capacity to hand out errands while additionally demonstrating that you went after a reasonable number of undertakings yourself. In the case of the charity event, you can specify that you could keep every other person in their place while additionally tracking and measuring gifts and making sense of the most ideal approach to attract attention.

Considering all of this, an example of an answer to this question could be: „As leader of my charity, I was in charge of a certain number of individuals. One of the greatest difficulties was assembling our yearly quota for ABC charity, which hasn't had the biggest success as of late. I sorted out many individuals, made a spreadsheet to track gifts and inspired a few nearby famous people to go to the event. At last, the diligent work didn't go to waste, and we had the best year yet as a result: We raised a certain amount of money for the philanthropy and also won several awards.“

Question number 22: Tell Me About a Time When You Failed

Whenever you have a job interview, you're probably going to hear questions such as, "tell me about a period when you failed."

Employers need to see that you're responsible and forthright, rather than rationalizing. Show them you assume responsibility for past oversights as opposed to putting the fault on others.

Next, they need to see that you can gain from your slip-ups and utilize the experience to improve. Everybody commits errors, however, no hiring director wants to employ someone who's going to continue rehashing similar mistakes again and again. That makes them go crazy. So ensure you demonstrate to them what you gained from the experience and how you utilized it to move forward.

Remain on track with your answer and make a point to tell an unmistakable, compact story. Whenever they pose a question that requires a story, they're hoping to see whether you can recount a reasonable story without getting diverted. So don't let your answers meander on for 5 minutes. Keep it on-track and brief. Portray the circumstance you were in, the decision you made, and how it turned out in a couple of minutes.

You'll generally get extra points from a hiring manager in the event that you sound humble, so attempt to do that too. Do this by seeming like you welcome the things you learned and are cheerful to have learned it despite the fact that encountering a failure isn't pleasant at the time. In the event that you do those things, you'll have an extraordinary answer that will awe the interviewer when they request that you portray a period you failed.

Try not to give your answer a chance to get muddled or continue for 3-4 minutes. Make sure to be compact and brief!

Likewise, don't make it seem like you didn't take in anything from the experience, and don't accuse others. Continuously be responsible for what you could have done any other way when it comes to failure.

Everybody flops, so don't attempt to shroud it or act like you don't fail. Set up an example and be prepared to discuss it.

Likewise, abstain from giving a story that makes you sound imprudent, or like somebody who hurries through things and commits numerous errors by and large. Employing managers aren't going to want to enlist somebody who appears as though they surge and commit errors as often as possible.

It's smarter to recount a story that demonstrates a one-time slip-up or mistake, as opposed to a reoccurring issue.

I wouldn't suggest discussing a tremendous catastrophe. On the off chance that you committed a monstrous error that cost a past organization a lot of money, I'd stay silent and locate a "less frightening" story.

An example of an answer to this question would be: „I was dealing with an undertaking for one of our greatest customers in my past organization, and I was so anxious to satisfy them that I revealed to them we could complete the task within 7 days.

I thought this was feasible, yet it wound up taking 2 weeks and they were not upbeat. Thinking back, I understood I ought to have been increasingly preservationist in my promise to the customer. I understood that a customer won't be disturbed in case you're clear about the course of events ahead of time, yet they will be baffled on the off chance that you guarantee something and it doesn't turn out according to that.

So I took this experience and utilized it to wind up much better at dealing with the desires for customers amid tasks I direct. For instance, on the following venture with an alternate customer, I disclosed to them it'd take a month and we completed in 3 weeks. They were exceptionally glad about this."

Question number 23: What Have You Learned on Your Previous Jobs?

Recognizing what you achieved at past employment will enable an interviewer to comprehend what you can add to this organization. In this way, it is truly frequent to be asked, "What have you learned from previous jobs?"

Note that you are not being asked what you did at your last occupation. Rather, you are being asked about what abilities you developed, what you found out about yourself and what you found out about the business from earlier occupations. Having effectively learned key abilities will make you exceptionally alluring in a job interview, and it can give you a truly necessary advantage to emerge from the group.

When discussing past locations of work, there are sure things to underscore in your answer. Talk about business and individual abilities you have learned. Turn any negative encounters into positive ones. Talk about abilities that are important to the position you are competing for. Adjust your response to the estimations of the organization.

There is a ton you learn with any job, however, so as to abstain from giving a protracted, indulgent answer, you should simply concentrate on a few things that will help you in the new job.

Not understanding the question can result in a not exactly excellent answer, so prepare and avoid committing these regular errors. Abstain from discussing things you discovered that won't generally assist you with this new job. Try not to concentrate on only business skills or only on personal skills. Avoid badmouthing and talking against a past job. Try not to say that there isn't anything you learned. There is something to be picked up from each professional training, and on the off chance that you can't recall anything, invest some time and energy before the meeting contemplating it with the goal of being prepared.

A smart response to a question in regards to aptitudes you gained from your last occupation should look something like this: "When I began my last employment, I just had an essential comprehension of the basics of SEO, however at this point I have figured out how to run a profitable PPC campaign and how to successfully use online networking pages. I additionally didn't have much involvement with public speaking, yet at my last employment, I needed to give a few gathering introductions, and thus, I believe I have turned out to be greatly improved at conveying information proficiently."

Question number 24: What is Your Greatest Accomplishment?

What's the most ideal approach to answering the question concerning your accomplishments and achievements? this can be an intense question to reply to. It's hard in case you're fresh alumni without a lot to draw from, and it's considerably harder when thinking back on a bunch of tiny achievements through the span of your career.

Moreover, you may not by any means view your most prominent accomplishment as business related; you should seriously mull over it to be an occasion in your private life like working with a mentally unbalanced youngster or defeating a personal impediment. Here are a few strategies to answer inquiries regarding your most noteworthy achievements:

Start off with a story. Portray the test you were facing, your plan for tackling it and the achievement you saw as the result.

Concentrate on accomplishments. Did you win a horse race or a chess rivalry? Lose a certain amount of weight? Without a doubt, that is amazing and demonstrates that you are committed and a diligent employee, yet except if the interviewer explicitly wants some information about your most noteworthy achievement outside of work, center around accomplishments that exhibit that you're a really great candidate for the position.

Try not to endeavor to be entertaining, senseless or charming. Consider the question important and answer it expertly. Try not to talk bad about another person trying to make yourself seem better and keep your story constructive.

Mention an ongoing and recent achievement. Indeed, getting the whole organization snared to a server as opposed to dial-up network access was an achievement in those days; today, not all that significant.

As usual, be straightforward. Try not to be enticed to embellish the reality or make a case for an accomplishment that wasn't yours. Deceptive nature amid the job interview procedure has a way for causing issues down the road for employment searchers, at times long after they've found the activity. (In the case of nothing else, you'd need to live with the dread that your lie would be found!)

Utilize your response to show explicit aptitudes or characteristics that you know the hiring manager is searching for. It is a decent chance to coordinate your capabilities to the activity and show that you're a really amazing contender for the position. Look past hard aptitudes; exhibiting that you're a superb communicator, a patient individual or a propelled and adaptable colleague will inspire the interviewer.

Draw an obvious conclusion. Utilize the chance to relate what you've achieved to the position you're applying for when you've been given the floor to boast and hotshot how your accomplishment could help the organization in the event that you were procured. Make it simple for the interviewer to see what you're trying to convey.

An example of an answer to this question could be: "I'm most glad for my work in my last internship. I got the opportunity to help build up another Android application for a quickly developing startup and I led the pack on the venture after one of the other colleagues quit. This was outside the first extent of my temporary job, however, it wound up being an extraordinary chance to learn and demonstrate what I'm prepared to do. I managed to deliver the application on time before the cancellation of my temporary job ie. internship, and have sent it to the online store. It as of now has 25,000 clients and a good number of positive reviews. I can send you the URL in case you're intrigued"

Question number 25: What is The Most Difficult Decision You Have Made?

Comparable interview questions are: What do you do when you have to make a hard decision? Provide me with an example of your decision-making thought process. What is your manner of thinking in working through an intense choice? When is it most troublesome for you to decide?

The interviewer needs to discover both what you consider to be your hardest choice and how/why you settled on that choice. In spite of the fact that the question is just getting some information about the choice itself, the interviewer will ordinarily want to dive deep into the subtleties around what hinted at the need to settle on the choice, the procedure you used for the choice and the inevitable result and additionally aftermath of the choice.

While you might be enticed to discuss an individual choice in your life, this isn't the correct setting for doing so. Go with a business choice in your work or, for undergrads with next to zero work understanding, you can discuss a choice identified with your scholarly work. You ought to be ready to discuss what was involved in making the choice, how you settled on the choice and what result was accomplished.

This is your opportunity to demonstrate you're capable of using sound judgment in testing circumstances. Begin with a story that demonstrates you were effective in taking care of an extreme issue and that demonstrates a positive outcome for your supervisor and the business. Whatever model you use, ensure it features a quality you would convey to the job.

The interviewer is keen on figuring out how you think. Assume their perspective. Every job has its problems, and they need to realize you'll be intentional and cautious in gauging the alternatives.

A progressively experienced competitor could answer this way: "Most likely the hardest choice I've needed to make was the point at which I moved from my earlier group to my present group at work. I had gone through two years working with my earlier group and we had achieved a lot amid that time. The chief of the other office reached out to me to inquire as to whether I would be keen on the new job and, at first, I declined. Nonetheless, she conversed with me further about how it would be an opportunity which would give me an open door for quickened proficient development."

A case of an answer that an entry-level candidate would provide is: "My hardest choice was changing majors to my present major in my Sophomore year. I had taken my unique major because of impact from others, however, amid my Freshman year, I took a sequence of profession tests and came to the conclusion that my capabilities, identity and my interests were more suited for my current field. Changing majors implied I would need to take a heavier class stack, which could affect my evaluations. Be that as it may, I have possessed the capacity to keep up my high GPA all through college and I was even as of late given an honor for the best understudy in my major."

Question Number 26: Do You Prefer Working Alone or in a Group?

"Would you rather ˎwork as a part of the team or alone?" can be a precarious job interview question to reply to, particularly when you're applying for a remote job. While it might appear as though there's one answer that would make the hiring manager happy, there truly are positives and negatives regardless of which way you reply.

In the event that you state that you are a cooperative person, this may appear the undeniable answer. All things considered, coordinated effort is a key piece of an effective group, and you could accept that your manager needs to ensure that you can function admirably with your different associates. They don't need somebody who will be introverted or problematic amid gatherings, you may think. Thing is, the hiring chief may interpret this as a sign that you require other individuals' info, counsel, and help to complete your very own work. It might likewise reveal to them that you wouldn't almost certainly prevail by working autonomously, in a remote situation, which could be a colossal warning for the hiring manager.

Regardless of whether you want to work without anyone else's input, you may be reluctant to state so during the interview. By picking this alternative, you envision that your manager-to-be is believing that you'll be squatted in your home office, disagreeable and reluctant to partake with your kindred partners. By picking this decision, you may imagine that you are communicating something specific that you don't care for individuals and would want to work alone. Or then again, on the other side, you may answer along these lines to demonstrate that you can self-oversee and take care of business without a ton of hand-holding or support.

Call attention to the positives of both. One great approach to answering this inquiry is to join the positive parts of the two choices. You can say something like, "I appreciate both. I can work both in a group, and work alone. Contingent upon the venture that should be done, I can work autonomously to finish my undertakings on time, however, I likewise appreciate conceptualizing and teaming up with my partners." That way, your potential supervisor understands that you like a group situation, yet you can work freely also. Emphasize your inclination, however, clarify that you're adaptable.

The subject of whether you like to deal with a group or alone is truly used to decide whether you're a social butterfly or a contemplative person and how that identity type may possibly influence your work execution in a remote workplace. In case you're an introvert, you can say that you by and large appreciate working alone, yet clarify that you can likewise cooperate with other people, as well. For instance, "I truly appreciate working together with a group and conceptualizing thoughts, however that doesn't mean I can't work freely to complete things. Generally, I incline toward working autonomously so as to comply with my time constraints, however, I appreciate teaming up in a gathering to start new thoughts."

Refer to the job description. It may be expressed that you would work prevalently freely and that may be definitely fit for your abilities! At the point when asked which way you like to work, you can refer to the job description as a feature of your answer. You can say, "I read in the job description that the ideal job candidate would most likely work autonomously, and that particularly fits with the manner in which I do my best work, as well."

Suppose that it's not clearly expressed which identity type (i.e., outgoing individual or thoughtful person) would be best for the activity. All things considered, you should attempt to choose early which of these methods for working is most required for the job to which you're applying for. Make an effort to comprehend your qualities and how you really do like to do things, so you can answer sincerely and thoughtfully.

On the off chance that you run across this question amid your prospective job interview, remember that you don't need to pick one alternative over another. In the event that you delineate the advantages of both working alone and in a group, your supervisor will see that you are a flexible occupation competitor who might be an incredible expansion to his organization.

Question Number 27: Do You Have Any Questions for Me/Us?

Your prospective job interview is practically finished and the procuring supervisor has given you a ton of significant data about the position. As the discussion is nearing its conclusion, they ask, "Do you have any questions for me?"

This question is normally solicited toward the end from meetings and it is a basically vital piece of the discussion. Oppose the impulse to state no, regardless of whether you're sure the job is a decent counterpart for you. Actually, interviewers anticipate that you should have some questions. it shows that you're interested and genuine about the job opening.

It is imperative to make your questions good since that demonstrates that you are intrigued. Your interview gives the procuring chief knowledge into your expert experience, capabilities, and achievements, but on the other hand, it's an extraordinary time for you to become familiar with the organization and occupation. Concentrate on making inquiries about points that weren't discussed, or subjects you might want to talk about in more prominent detail.

By posing good questions you are likewise demonstrating your advantage. Making sure to ask attentive questions in your interview showcases your enthusiasm for the job opening. It likewise demonstrates the procuring director that you've considered what it means to be working this job at this organization. With the correct questions, you'll have the capacity to represent your insight into the organization and industry, alongside your drive to exceed expectations in the new position.

Making sure to ask great questions since that leaves a positive last impression. Making it to the interviewing stage is as of now a sign that you're the best applicant. With astute questions, you can keep on emerging from different candidates and show that you're an extraordinary fit for the job.

Since the hiring supervisor will cover a great deal of data during the interview and may unwittingly answer the inquiries you intend to ask, consider writing down up to 10 questions. You might need to record your questions in a notepad or portfolio that you take with you to the meeting. Allude to this list when the interviewer asks, "Do you have any questions for us?" and select a few questions that weren't answered before. Pick those questions that show and exhibit how you were locked in and tuning in and the ones that can enable you to become familiar with the job opening.

Doing your research and your homework about the organization is a simple method to comprehend the organization's history, mission statement and qualities. An extraordinary place to begin is by looking up the organization's site. You can likewise look the web for ongoing articles. Utilize the data you find to form your questions. Your drive will be generally welcomed in light of the fact that it demonstrates you put in the effort to find out about the organization and its industry.

Think about this whole process as a discussion between yourself and the procuring manager. Rehearsing your questions for them ahead of time can make you progressively agreeable and give you some certainty and help on the day of the interview. Invest energy in a calm place practicing your questions before a mirror or with a companion or relative.

The hiring supervisor may have officially mentioned information about the activities and capacities, yet this is the perfect time to get more insights regarding the everyday duties, desires, and objectives. You could ask: What does a run of the mill day look like for an individual in this position? What are your short and long haul objectives for a candidate such as yourself? How has this job developed or adjusted to suit the requirements of the company as a whole?

Making sure to pose questions about the organization uncovers that you've done your examination and gives you superior insight into the organization's viewpoint, qualities and culture. Besides, it gives the feeling that you're keen on developing with the organization in the long haul. Think about asking: „Why do you appreciate working here?" „How might you depict the organization's way of life?" „ What sort of development does the organization hope to see inside the following five years?" „Would you be able to portray a portion of the organization's ongoing difficulties and accomplishments?"

Ensure the enlisting manager doesn't leave questions unanswered regarding your capabilities. On the off chance that they do, this is a prime time to underline how your abilities line up with the job. These kinds of questions could be like these: „What characteristics do you search for in an applicant?" „ Do you have any worries about my experience or range of abilities?" „ Are there reservations in regards to my fit with the job or organization?"

Spare your last questions to ask about the continuation in the employing procedure. You'll pass on your enthusiasm for the position one final time as well as finding out about the contracting timetable, potential extra opportunities or when you can hope to get notification from them. You may state:

"I'm truly delighted in getting familiar with this opportunity. What are the subsequent stages in the hiring procedure?"

"Much obliged to you for disclosing the job to me in such profundity. When may I expect to hear from you again?"

Conclusion

It's necessary to conclude your job interview while leaving a favorable final impression, and that involves saying goodbye to the hiring manager properly and settling the business meeting in a way that will positively impact the future.

Final impressions can be the most enduring and they are just as important as the first impressions since people remember the beginning and the most. That being said, you should give some thought beforehand to how you will conclude the interview.

Remember that finishing an interview is a great chance to showcase your enthusiasm for the job position. One way to achieve this is to say how the interviewing process has confirmed your enthusiasm for the job. For example, you could say in the end, "I'm really thankful for the opportunity to be more informed about this job. Working with the cutting edge technology that your firm utilizes and the new products and services have definitely boosted my desire to assume a leadership role with one of your project teams."

If you are certain that you want to get the job, after the interview has ended, do what any good businessperson would do and ask for the job, albeit with some subtlety. You could say, "I wish to let you know that I am quite interested in playing part in your firm, and I do sincerely hope that you will be offering me a spot during next session of interviews. Please, let me know if you will have any additional questions for me in the future."

The conclusion of your interview also is a good chance to emphasize why the jobs fit your skills and qualifications and is compatible considering your assets. You could say something along the lines of, "In closing, it appears to me that this job would fit me well. I am excited to use my advanced SEO skills, expertise in managing projects and ability to complete projects within a deadline."

Before exiting the interview, make sure you sure you have accurate expectations with the hiring process. Ask about the timeframe for making a final decision and if there will be other levels of the interviewing so that you can be ready for any follow up questions and requests.

Right after the interview has ended, take notes about the meeting itself while you remember as much as possible. Create your email as soon as you can in which you will influence the evaluation of your candidacy while there is still time.

I hope that you have enjoyed reading through this book and that you have found it useful and that applying what you read will ensure that you get that job that you want. If you wish to share your thought and your results and your stories, then you can do so by leaving a review on the Amazon page.

Made in the USA
Coppell, TX
05 November 2020